A Sense of Science

Exploring Animal Life

Claire Llewellyn

W

FRANKLIN WATTS
LONDON·SYDNEY

First published in 2007 by
Franklin Watts
338 Euston Road
London NW1 3BH

Franklin Watts Australia
Level 17/207 Kent Street
Sydney NSW 2000

Editor: Jeremy Smith
Art Director: Jonathan Hair
Design: Matthew Lilly
Cover and design concept:
Jonathan Hair

Photograph credits: Steve Shott
except: Alamy: 7b, 15t, 17t, 25b.
Corbis: 4, 12, 24, 27.
istockphoto: 8, 9t, 10, 11b, 13, 16b, 17b,
18-19 all, 25t.

A CIP catalogue record
for this book is available
from the British Library.

Dewey classification: 590

ISBN: 978 0 7496 7048 1

Printed in China

Franklin Watts is a division of
Hachette Children's Books.

Contents

A world of animals

Animals live
in the world around us.

Crabs live by the seashore.

Which animals do you see where you live?

Rabbits live
in fields.

We are animals too.

An animal's body

Animals' bodies are different from ours. A cat has fur all over its body.

Always wash your hands after touching an animal.

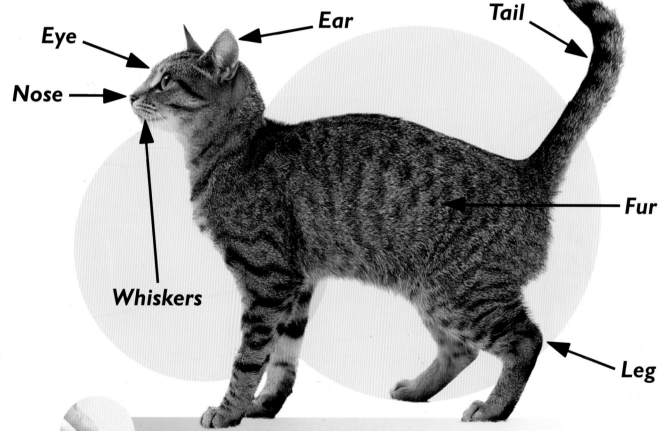

Eye

Nose

Ear

Tail

Fur

Whiskers

Leg

Touchy-feely

Have you ever touched any animals? What did they feel like?

A bird has feathers and wings.

Feathers

Wing

Eye

Beak

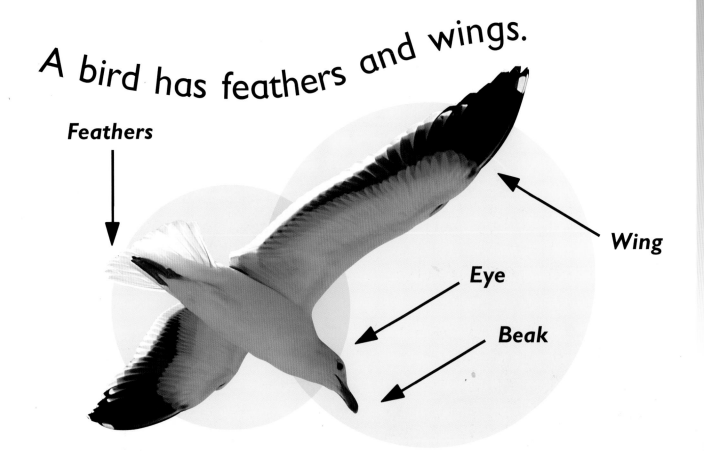

Fin

Scales

A fish is covered with shiny scales.

Eye

Tail

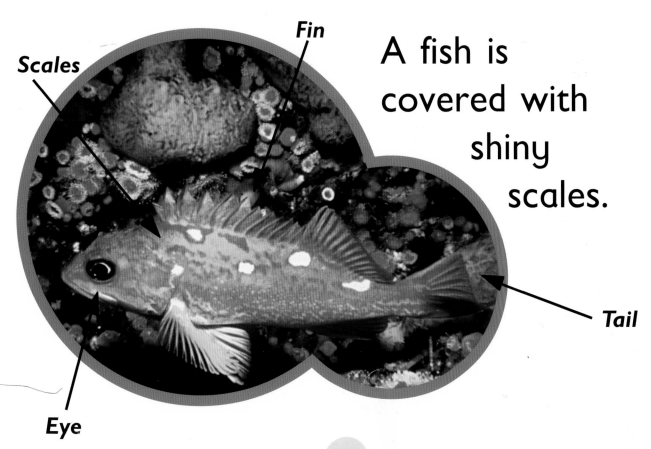

On the move

Animals move in many different ways.

A butterfly flaps its wings to fly through the air.

Animal spotter

Have a look for some animals outside. How are they moving?

A horse runs on its
four long legs.

A snake wriggles along the ground.

Meal time

All animals
need food and
water to live.

Insect I-spy
Watch bees and
butterflies on a
warm, sunny day.
Where do they
feed?

A spider eats insects
that it catches in its web.

A squirrel feeds
on nuts.

This owl
has caught
a mouse.

Baby animals

All animals
have young.

Baby talk
Look at the young
animals in this picutres.
What noises, if any, do
they make?

This pig has had a piglet.

14

This mouse is looking after her young.

This caterpillar can look after itself. One day it will change into a butterfly.

Growing up

Baby animals change as they grow older.

Lambs grow bigger and stronger.

Young birds
learn to fly.

Getting bigger
We grow, too.
How much taller
than you are your
mum and dad?

When this kitten plays it is learning to hunt.

Changing shape

Some animals change shape as they grow up.

A frog's eggs hatch into tiny tadpoles.

tadpole

egg

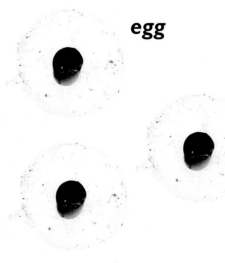

Look and learn

Look at the frog's eggs. How are they different from a bird's eggs?

tadpole with back legs

As a tadpole gets bigger it grows legs.

tadpole with front and back legs

The tadpole changes into a frog. It is an adult.

frog

Animal senses

Animals use their senses to find out about the world around them.

Sense it!
How do you use your eyes, ears and nose to find out about the world around you?

A deer's ears help it to hear danger.

A cat's eyes help it to see at night.

A chicken can hear worms under the soil.

A fox can smell food from a long way away!

On the farm

Some animals live on farms.

A farmer gives his cattle food and shelter.

Good to eat

Look at the food inside your fridge.
Did any of it come from farm animals?

Sheep give us wool, milk and meat.

Chickens give us eggs and meat.

Animals at home

Pet animals
live in our homes.

We feed
and look
after our
pets.

Other animals live in our homes, too.

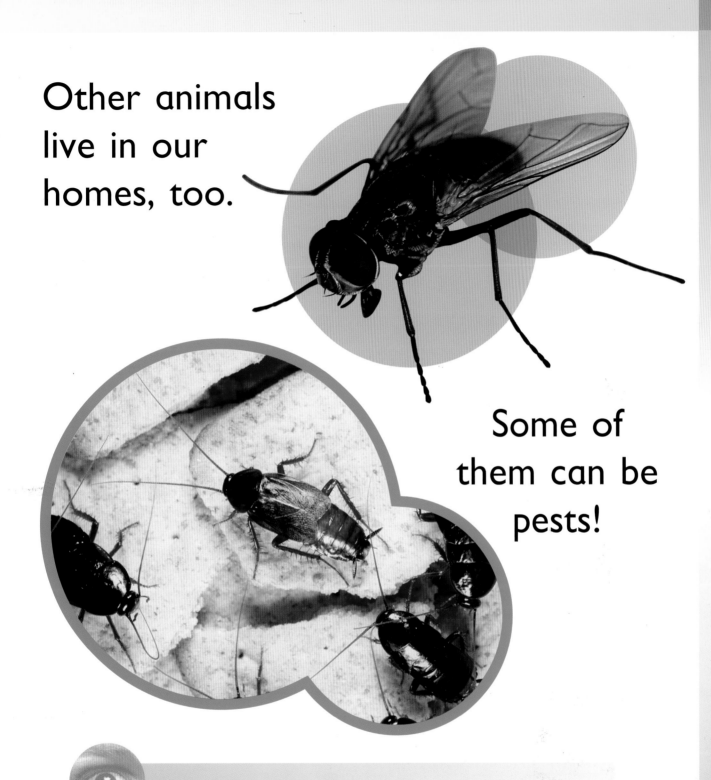

Some of them can be pests!

Creepy-crawly
Which small animals live in your home? Look around and see.

Caring for animals

Animals are living things.

We need to treat them with care.

We must look
after the places
where animals live.

Winter watch

Put out food
and water for
the birds in
winter. Which
birds come
to feed?

Never drop litter.
It can harm wild animals.

Glossary

Claw
The sharp nail on the toe of an animal.

Fur
The hair that covers an animal's body.

Insects
A group of animals that are usually small and have six legs.

Litter
Rubbish that we throw on the ground.

Pest
An animal that eats our plants or spoils our food.

Scales
The small, flat pieces that cover a fish's body.

Senses
The five different ways that our body tells us about the world around us – by seeing, hearing, feeling, tasting and smelling.

Shelter
A dry place to live.

Web
Sticky trap made by a spider.

Whiskers
Long fine hairs on the face of some animals.

Make a creepy-crawly trap

1. Find a glass jar. Put some leaves and earth in it and some scraps of apple, lettuce, tomato or cheese.

---

2. Sink the jar in the ground to soil level. Put a piece of wood on top of two stones to stop rain getting into the jar.

3. Check your trap every day to see what you have caught. Try to find out the animals' names. Draw them and then let them go.

---

4. Put your trap in wet and dry places. Do you catch the same animals in each place?

Index

BUSY PLACES

Airport

Harriet Hains
With thanks to Stansted Airport

W
FRANKLIN WATTS
NEW YORK • LONDON • SYDNEY

It's 10 a.m. at the airport. Everyone is busy as there are planes taking off and landing all the time.

Inside the airport building people are arriving for their flights or collecting friends. Other people are making sure that everything runs smoothly.

Welcome to London Stansted

B·A·A

At the information desk
Mr Evans asks for help.
The officer speaks into
the microphone.
"Can Mrs Evans meet her
husband at the information
desk," he says.

Rona is flying to Italy. She looks at the departure board. "My flight leaves in one hour," she says to herself.

Police officers walk around the airport to make sure it is safe for the passengers.

4

Rona changes some of her English money into Italian money ready for when she gets there. "Can I have some Italian 'lire', please?" she asks the woman at the exchange office.

Next Rona goes
to the shop to
choose a magazine
to read on the flight.
"Now I can relax
and have a cup of
coffee," she thinks.

Meanwhile the Frost family are 'checking-in' at the desk.

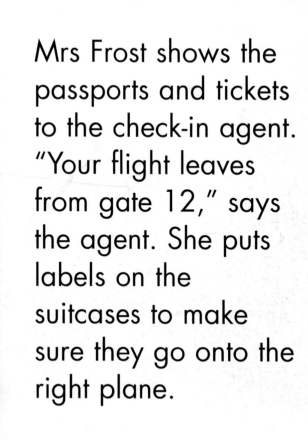

Mrs Frost shows the passports and tickets to the check-in agent. "Your flight leaves from gate 12," says the agent. She puts labels on the suitcases to make sure they go onto the right plane.

7

The Frosts walk to the departure lounge to wait for their flight. Before they get on the plane their luggage must be put through an X-ray machine to check that it is safe.

Next, one by one, the Frost family walk through another machine. This makes a beeping sound when it detects metal. "Beep, beep," goes the machine. "Are you wearing a metal watch?" the security guard asks Riley.

A plane has just landed
and the passengers are
getting off. Their luggage
is put onto trucks and
then on a conveyor belt.
This carries the luggage
into the airport for the
passengers to collect.

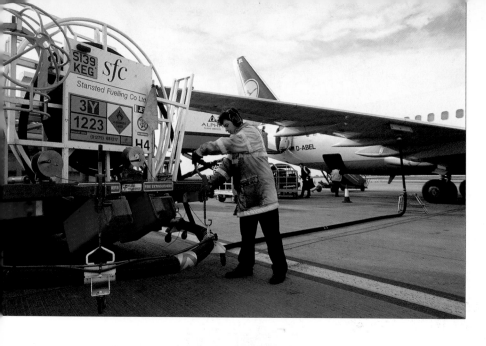

The ground
crew get the
plane ready for
its next flight.
They pump
fuel into the
tanks and
check the tyres.

A large truck brings the passengers' meals and snacks to the plane. The container is lifted up so that the food can be put on board.

Meanwhile, the captain and the co-pilot check the weather for their flight. "It looks clear and bright," says the captain.

As soon as the plane is ready for the flight, the captain and crew make their way across the tarmac.

At last it's time for the passengers
to board the plane, too.
"Here we go!" says Mrs Frost as they
go through the boarding gate.

In the control tower the air traffic controllers make sure the planes land and take off safely. "You are cleared for take-off," says the controller.

The airfield ranger fires a safety pistol into the air to scare any birds that are around. It is important that the runway is clear and safe for take-off.

Nearby, fire engines are ready in case there is an accident. One crew practise a 'call out'. "Let's go through that again," says the chief.

At 4 p.m. a plane arrives from Germany. The marshaller shows the captain where to park the plane. She uses paddles so that he can see clearly.

The plane is parked in position. Then the passengers walk through a tunnel. The tunnel is attached to the door of the plane.

Louise has just arrived on the plane from Germany. First the officer at passport control checks her passport. "That's fine, thank you!" the officer says.

Next Louise collects her luggage from the conveyor belt.

Then she shows her bag to a customs officer. "No problems here, thank you," he says. "Enjoy the rest of your journey home."

21

Now Louise can walk out through the airport and get a taxi home.

Care and safety in an airport

When you are in a busy place it is important to make sure that you and others keep safe.

Try to remember some of these tips:

1. Always stay close to your parent or adult friend.

2. Keep your hand luggage with you all the time.

3. Take something to read or do quietly while you are waiting for your plane.

4. Do not touch anything that does not belong to you.

5. Never take computer games, radios or personal stereos on a plane as they may stop the plane's equipment from working properly.

Index

© 1999 Franklin Watts
96 Leonard Street
London
EC2A 4RH

Franklin Watts Australia
14 Mars Road
Lane Cove
NSW 2066

ISBN 0 7496 3339 5

Dewey Decimal Classification Number
387.7

A CIP catalogue record for this book is
available from the British Library

Printed in Hong Kong

Editor: Samantha Armstrong
Designer: Louise Snowdon
Photographer: Chris Fairclough
Illustrations: Nick Ward

With thanks to all at Stansted Airport,
Go, Rona Young, Louise Fitzpatrick,
Martin Shulton and Deana, Ellis and
Riley Frost.

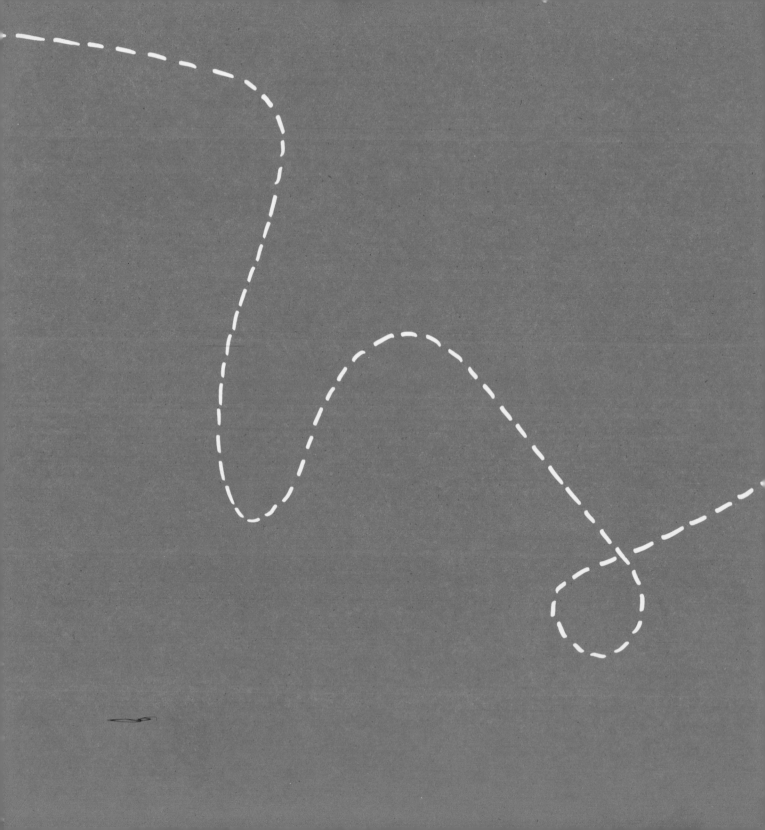